Too Wise
to Want to Be
Young Again

To Tamara, my mother,
who at 92 shows me every day
how to age with grace
and dignity.

Too Wise to Want to Be Young Again

A Witty View of How to Stop Counting the Years and Start Living Them

Natasha Josefowitz, Ph.D.

Blue Mountain Press ®

SPS Studios™
Boulder, Colorado

Copyright © 1995 by Natasha Josefowitz.
Copyright © 1995 by Blue Mountain Arts, Inc.

Library of Congress Catalog Card Number: 95-25077
ISBN: 0-88396-422-8

⊓⊓ design on book cover is registered in
U.S. Patent and Trademark Office.

Some of the poems in this volume have previously appeared in the following books published by Warner Books: **Natasha's Words for Lovers, Natasha's Words for Families, Natasha's Words for Friends,** and **Is This Where I Was Going?** by Natasha Josefowitz.

Manufactured in the United States of America
Sixth Printing: February 2000

♲ This book is printed on recycled paper.

Library of Congress Cataloging-in-Publication Data
Josefowitz, Natasha.
    Too wise to want to be young again : a witty view of how to stop
  counting the years and start living them / Natasha Josefowitz.
        p.   cm.
    ISBN 0-88396-422-8
    1. Aging--Poetry.   I. Title.
  PS3560.0768T66   1995
  813' .54--dc20   95-25077
                                                             CIP

SPS Studios, Inc.
P.O. Box 4549, Boulder, Colorado 80306

CONTENTS

INTRODUCTION

Times are changing! We are about to have more "senior citizens" in this country than ever before. Products, advertising, entertainment, and services are becoming more focused on this older generation. It is a wonderful time to grow older.

Yes, our world is being transformed around us faster than ever, and we need to evolve with it. Men have learned to change diapers, and women can be construction workers. We have exchanged household help for food processors, cooking for take-out, and leisurely dining for fast foods. We used to read more, listen to the radio, and write letters; now we watch TV, talk on the telephone, and fax.

It is written that there is "a time to weep and a time to laugh." The trick is to know which one to do when. Given a choice, let's go with the laughter.

Chapter 1

THE GOOD NEWS IS...

WE DON'T HAVE TO TRY TO BE PERFECT ANYMORE!

My last New Year's resolution was, "I don't plan to improve this year." Not being perfect in every way is good enough.

So what if we have a few wrinkles, our hair is greying, and we move a little slower. We have earned every one of those wrinkles. In our youth, we may have had more energy, but it was scattered over many pursuits. Now our energy is well focused on a few significant undertakings. We are like fine wine... the older we get, the more mellow and richer flavored we become.

We celebrate our increased wisdom and our increased capacity to love life as we realize that we truly belong to this earth, just as it belongs to us.

I'm not okay,
    you're not okay,
and that's okay!

You're Only As Old As You Think You Are

This is a time in my life
that I don't want to miss —
old age is a privilege
denied to a lot of people
and the best way to avoid
becoming an old dog
is to keep learning
new tricks

I always say that age
is only important
if you happen to be
wine or cheese
Yet when I get out of the shower
I am relieved that the mirror
is all fogged up
I have also noticed that
I'm beginning to decline a lot of offers —
preferring to stay home —
which is probably why they
call these the "declining years"

After middle-age spread
I look forward to old-age shrinkage
and I'm much too wise
to ever want to be young again

The Best Is Yet to Come

Don't have to climb
the corporate ladder
don't have to be upwardly mobile
don't have to move mountains
don't have to compete
or struggle with others
don't have to set my sights
upon some distant goal
don't have to prove anything
or cater to anyone
It's not uphill anymore
It's over that hill
with a lovely view
of the best years
yet to come

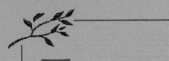

There's Always Something
I Must Do First

*I will start enjoying life
after I get myself organized*

*I will exercise more
after I have updated my filing system*

*I will take a vacation
after I clean out the attic*

*I will buy myself some nice clothes
after I lose some weight*

*I will spend more time with my family
after I finish pasting the pictures
in the photo albums*

*I will start enjoying life
after it is too late*

NOT !!!

I Finally Have Time

I now have time
for reading a newspaper
cover to cover instead of
skimming through it for the news

I can take a leisurely stroll
go to an afternoon movie
attend a lecture at the museum
enroll in a course
on something totally unrelated
to professional development

I have time to chat with a friend
about absolutely nothing
take the grandchildren for an outing
and be there for the children
when they need me

I read magazines
that are not educational
take time to shop
when I don't need anything
cook from scratch
instead of relying on take-out

I can wait at the light
without honking my horn
I don't cut people off
because I'm rushing somewhere
don't look at my watch
every minute and groan

I'm not afraid of wasting time
for I finally have time
to take... my time

These Are the Years
of Living Dangerously

I drank milk
the day after its expiration date

I talked to the bus driver
while the bus was in motion

I undid my safety belt
before the plane came to a complete stop

I did not brush my teeth
before going to bed

I went out without my umbrella
even though they predicted rain

I took off the tag on my pillow that says
"Do not remove"

I walked where it said
"Do not step on the grass"

I took my dog out
without a leash

I washed a garment that said
"Dry-clean only"

I picked a flower
in someone else's garden

I live dangerously

That's Me!

It's the crow's-feet
around my eyes
and the puffiness
below them.

It's the furrows
on my forehead
and the wrinkles
on my neck

that make me
place my hands
upon my temples,
pull back and say:
"See, this is how I would
look with a face-lift."

And a face
ten years younger appears,
but it's not mine.
Then I let go
and smile at the familiar one,
knowing that's me
trying to grow older
gracefully.

Why Should I Worry?

The young people don't worry when they...

don't remember
their best friend's name,

lose their car keys twice a week,

can't find their wallets,

misplace their glasses,

walk into a room and don't know
what it was they were looking for,

forget their own phone number,

can't think of a common word
they use every day,

can't recall what they just read
or what someone just said,

lose the list they wrote of
things to remember.

The young people just shrug their shoulders,
but people my age
think they have Alzheimer's disease.

Chapter 2

SOME THINGS NEVER CHANGE

I am different from when I was young: wiser, less hassled by little things, quieter inside, more outspoken, more appreciative. Yet I'm also the same. The values I was raised with still hold true for me. What I learned from my parents, I taught my children who are teaching their children. Although in many ways I am better than I used to be, there is a basic core that I recognize throughout my life. I continue to be spontaneous, even in situations where it is inappropriate; I remain anxious when my husband is late coming home; I give advice to my children even when it is not solicited. So even when I know better, I remain true to myself, because some things never change.

Tomorrow I Will Change

Tomorrow I will change
turn a new leaf
become this new person

I will exercise before breakfast
not eat cookies between meals
not fret over trivialities
not run about
getting upset
that I'm not getting
everything done

Tomorrow I will change

I say this every day

My Closet Is Full of Nothing to Wear

*Although my closet is full
I have nothing to wear
My clothes come in different sizes
waiting for me to lose weight
while in the meantime
I have nothing to wear*

*I have a lot of shoes
some of which I keep only
for when it might rain
as I wouldn't want to ruin
a perfectly good pair*

*I own too many purses
but they match
my many shoes*

*I have hats I never wear
but they might become
fashionable again someday*

*There is a drawer full of scarves
That is because they never wear out*

*The belts that are hanging
are too tight right now
but may fit again next year*

*So I stand
staring at a closet full
of nothing to wear*

My Mother Still Tells Me What to Do

My mother tells me that
it's cold today
I ought to wear a sweater
or it might rain
I should take an umbrella
or my dress is unbecoming
and my hair doesn't look right

She also says that
I should lose a few pounds
put cream on my face
wear a hat in the sun
not use swearwords
and stand up straight

My mother treats me like a child
She has not noticed that
I am now almost her age
and catching up fast

My mother tells me what to do
and always seems startled
when I tell her
I'm a grandmother, too

Photo Albums

The photos are in shoe boxes
dating several years back
Someday I'll have time
to put them in the photo albums

But as I look through them
I cannot remember
which grandchild it is
at age one week
or from which mountaintop
I wave on my skis

I cannot recall
which party we're smiling from
or who these people are
we seem to be so fond of

The photos in the shoe boxes
are waiting to be organized
chronologically
waiting to be pasted in
an orderly fashion
into the empty albums
purchased for that purpose
several years ago

I must fulfill
my task as the record keeper
of family events

I must preserve our pictorial history
someday
when I have time

Irresistible

I don't know why I take
the hotel stationery
why I take
the leftover soap
and pack their shower cap
when I have my own
why I keep the shampoos
and herbal bath packets
when I never use them at home

I guess when something's free
I just can't let it be

I'm not sure this is normal behavior
and I'm embarrassed to admit
that I have
a lot of hotel stationery
shower caps, soap, shampoo
and herbal bath packets at home
waiting for someone to use them

The Fear Never Stops

A dirt road
a woman walking
with a basket on her head

A field
a woman walking
with a bushel on her back

A city street
a woman walking
with a briefcase

A parking lot
a woman walking
with a grocery bag

A suburban mall
a woman walking
with a stroller

Suddenly
heavy footsteps behind her
Her heart beats quicker
A robber, a rapist
a harasser, a killer?
Perhaps just a nice person?
But she's afraid

The sound
of a stranger's footsteps
is a universal
female experience
of fear

I Had a Robbery While I Was Out

They broke a window
and pried open the chest
They took all my jewelry
and escaped

People say I'm lucky
they didn't kill me
People say I'm lucky
they didn't vandalize
but somehow it doesn't
make me feel better

So I say to myself
it was only things
it was only stones
But it was my father's watch
and my grandmother's earrings
and the gold heart
I was saving for my daughter's baby

Things are not only objects
they are symbols of a past
reminders of events
memories of people
Things are a part of ourselves

And so I mourn my loss
with fantasies of finding it all
with wishes for revenge
while blaming myself for being careless
none of which helps

I was robbed by unknown people
who not only took my things
but also took my peace of mind
My house does not feel safe anymore
I startle at the smallest noises
and feel vulnerable —
afraid it might happen again

Clutter

I own so much stuff
that it's beginning to own me
I am my stuff's servant
I dust it, move it around
take it with me when I move

I have electrical appliances
and gadgets I never use
I have a slow cooker to cook slowly
a microwave to cook fast
a pasta maker, a crêpe pan
a fondue pot, and a drawer full of
egg slicers, apple corers
cheese graters, potato peelers
spoon holders, lemon squeezers
tea strainers, and nut choppers

I have stuff that I hold on to
for when my grandchildren grow up
and might want it
(my children didn't)
and stuff that I can't throw away
because it triggers a memory
Then there's the stuff
that might be useful someday —
plastic rain caps
sewing kits from hotels
ribbons, shoehorns, buttons
an old puzzle someone might
put together again

I have so much stuff
that I forget what I have
and when I need it
I forget where I put it
I have stuff to store stuff
Soon I'll have to leave
the car in the street
so I can stuff the garage
with all my stuff!

Chapter 3

PROGRESS!

The dictionary says that "progress" means "steady improvement." But is it an improvement that everything goes faster today? To me, real progress would be healthy, well-fed children and adults worldwide, living and loving in peace.

Appliances

*My appliances
are meant to
make my life easier*

*I cook faster
clean faster
write faster
get there faster
reach people faster
while pushing buttons
turning dials
spinning my wheels
making my world
go even faster*

right past me

This Is Progress?

When I was young,
we didn't have computer dating,
dual careers, house-husbands, day-care centers,
latchkey children, or birth-control pills.

I didn't own a ballpoint pen, tape deck,
pantyhose, electric blanket, dishwasher,
contact lenses, or permanent-press clothes.

I had never heard of split atoms, jet planes,
word processors, laser beams, credit cards,
frozen foods, or artificial hearts.

Who would have thought then that
sexual harassment would be against the law,
and grandparents could sue
for visitation rights?

I still remember when "hippie" meant large hips,
"pot" was something to cook in,
and "far out" meant a distance away.

I remember when "rock" was a stone,
"AIDS" meant helpers,
a "trip" was to go someplace,
and "drugs" were only bought in pharmacies.

In my day, "hang up"
was what you did to the phone,
"hardware" was bought in hardware stores,
and "software" wasn't even a word.

Back then, we got married first,
then lived together;
we had a husband before having a baby,
and we didn't believe
a man could walk on the moon.

Now I find myself trying
to keep up with the times —
learning about computers,
listening to music
that I don't understand the words to,
and seeing men who wear earrings.

As much as I try to keep up,
I often want to give up,
shake my head, throw up my hands,
and wish for the good old days!

I Was Born Yesterday, but I'm Dealing with Today

I was not raised
to deal with numbers
I was not brought up
to understand legal matters
I was not taught
how to fill out a tax return
I have no idea
how to fix a leaky faucet
or how to rewire anything

While the boys in my school
had shop
the girls
had sewing
While the boys did math
we cooked

It's different now
and that is good
but I who was born yesterday
must somehow learn
how to manage today

Transportation

My grandmother
in her horse and carriage
did not travel far and wide
but on her way
she had time to look

My mother
in her car
went a lot faster
but saw a lot less

I travel by plane
and see nothing at all

On Opening a Medicine Bottle

The people designing caps
for medicine bottles
must be twenty years old

First you must align the arrow on the cap
with the arrow on the bottle
except that the arrow is so faint
you can't see it
                - or -
You must push the cap down hard
before you twist it open
except that no matter how hard you push
nothing happens
                - or -
You must first take off
the plastic around the cap
except that it is so tight that
even scissors can't make a dent in it
                - or -
You must pry open the cap
by lifting it upward
except that all your nails break
your fingers get raw
and the bottle stays closed
                - or -
There is an arrow on top of the cap
that indicates the direction to twist it
except that when you twist as directed
the bottle locks up permanently

In other words, medicine bottles are indeed
childproof as well as people proof

Throwing it against a wall does not work
nor does stomping on it or cursing it
And calling on a neighbor won't help —
unless of course
the neighbor is twenty years old

Chronologically Disabled

When I get up in the morning
I feel stiff and achy, so I go to the doctor
who says it is just a little arthritis...
"Take an aspirin."

When I eat a rich meal
I get heartburn and pains in my chest,
so I go to the doctor
who says it is just indigestion...
"Take an antacid."

When my heart beats too fast
and skips a few beats, I go to the doctor
who says it happens sometimes...
"Not to worry about it."

When I can't fall asleep
or I wake up in the middle of the night,
I go to the doctor who says...
"Don't take a nap in the afternoon."

When I'm at a party
and everyone mumbles,
I go to the doctor who says...
"Loss of hearing in the higher ranges
is normal at your age."

When I can't read the phone book anymore,
I go to the doctor who says...
"Go to the drugstore
and buy a pair of glasses."

When I take a walk and my hip bothers me,
I go to the doctor
who says it is osteoarthritis...
"Keep walking."

When I don't feel well,
I go to the doctor who says...
"This is what being older feels like."

Shopping

I go to the supermarket
wearing my reading glasses
in order to see
the fine print at the bottom of
the boxes and cans

Even when I can decipher it
I still don't know whether
the ingredients listed
are safe or lethal

I try for low fat
high fiber
less meat
more carbohydrates
Dairy is up for grabs
depending on the latest
article I have read

I keep mixing up
my soluble and insoluble fibers
and can't remember
which foods are high in potassium
and therefore good
or high in phosphates
and therefore bad

I know dark leafy vegetables are important
anything orange is essential
and mold on peanuts can cause cancer

And so I remain forever undecided
between broccoli
and chocolate ice cream

I Worry About the World

I worry about the ozone layer and acid rain
I worry about the destruction
of the Amazon rain forest
about the possibility of a nuclear disaster
and the depletion of our fossil fuels
I worry about the endangered species
and the pollution of our oceans
about overpopulation and gang violence
about the famine in Africa
a war in the Middle East
the rise in teenage pregnancies
the hospital crisis, AIDS
the federal deficit
the abused children
the peace negotiations

I worry and feel so helpless
about our earth
our country, our streets

So in the meantime
I'll call my mother more often
be there for my family
look in on my neighbor
take care of a friend
support worthwhile causes
be honest and outspoken

In the meantime
what I can do is
start improving the world
in my own backyard

Chapter 4

LOVING

Growing older with a loving mate can be a wonderful time. By now, we have learned the pleasures of touching, talking, hugging, and kissing. We appreciate each other in new ways; we value and respect one another and enjoy the fruits of life together. With the children gone, companionship takes on new dimensions. We each know the other's most intimate thoughts and foibles. In a newer relationship, there might be some initial shyness about a less-than-perfect body, but one loves a person, not a body or a face, and so the face and the body become lovable.

Knowing

I love him because
I know him so well
I love him in spite of
knowing him that well

The Stages of Marriage

*In the first years of marriage
the children are small
She's into feeding schedules, diapers
and getting up at night
He's just at the beginning of his career*

*In the middle years of marriage
the children are older
He's into business travel
and working longer hours
She finally has some time
for herself and other pursuits*

*In the last years of marriage
they both have slowed down
and they're finally in sync
with each other*

Do You Remember?

Remember how
you loved me then
you love me better now

Remember how
we dreamed and planned
we're doing it all now

Remember how
we were so young
we both have wrinkles now

Remember when
the kids were small
grandchildren are here now

Remember how
we used to jog
we smell the flowers now

Remember how
we skied downhill
we ski cross-country now

Remember how
we ate at Mother's
the kids come to us now

Remember how
we rushed through life
we take our time now

Remember how
I loved you then
I love you better now

Come a Little Closer

Come a little closer
so we can kiss

Move a little closer
so our arms can hug

Get a little closer
so our bodies touch

Come a little closer
for this too
is making love

His Breathing

I listen to the night
the silence interrupted
only by the rhythmic sound
of his breathing

It is perhaps
the most comforting sound
in the world —
his breathing peacefully
next to me

No matter what happened
in the daylight hours
the night is secured
by his quiet respiration
for he is here with me

We're Wonderful

You are intelligent, loving
fun to be with
always there

You're understanding
sympathetic
always giving me good advice

You are sensitive
very honest
always knowing the way I feel

You are aware
of today's issues
always trying to be fair

You're wise and kind
you're wonderful
yet what I like best about you
is that you think
I'm wonderful, too

I Love
Growing Old with You

Your hair is grey
your face is wrinkled
your skin is sagging
here and there

You must wear glasses
when you're reading
and I talk louder
so you can hear

You're not as lean
you're not as firm
your step is slower
than it was before

You fall asleep
watching television
and need to nap
in the afternoon

I love you better
as you grow older
but I like best
growing old with you

Chapter 5

FINDING A BALANCE—

LIFE IN THE MIDDLE OF
GROWN CHILDREN, GRANDCHILDREN,
AND AGING PARENTS

One of our greatest riches as we grow older is the opportunity to have multi-generational experiences in our lives. But one of the hardest things we have to learn is how to balance family joys with personal needs. We want to spend time with our husbands and friends, we want to babysit the grandchildren, and we want to visit our parents more often, but we also have to remember to leave some time for ourselves. With the proper balance, these are the years when we truly can celebrate life!

What Am I?

*Somewhere between always giving to others
and always keeping it all to myself
I stand
Somehow between only caring for others
and only caring for me
I live
But when I am only for others
I ask
who will be for me?
And when I am only for me
then what am I?*

I Can't Believe My Children Are Middle-Aged Now

Even though my children are grown
they will always still be "my children"
and so it is with great amazement
that I see the numbers accumulate
on their birthdays

I don't know how my schoolboy son
got to be a businessman
or when he went from kid to father

I don't know how my giggly little daughter
got to be the mother of three
and a successful woman with a Ph.D.

I can believe
that my mother is in her nineties
I can accept
that I'm almost seventy
but what doesn't seem possible at all
is that my children are middle-aged

Yet when I see how well they're doing
and what good spouses and parents they are
they become the living proof
of the way they were raised
All in all, I did a pretty good job

It's Comforting
and It's Not

As I grow older
my children are beginning to act
as if they were my parents
They ask whether
I take my vitamins
worry when I have a sniffle
scold me when I get overly tired
call if they haven't heard from me
and generally are beginning to act
as if they were my parents

It's comforting and it's not

For as much as I mind
becoming my mother's mother
I mind becoming my children's child

I Still Talk to My Father

My father has been gone
for many years now.
And yet when something special
happens to me,
I need to tell him about it.
I talk to him secretly
not really knowing
whether he hears,
but it makes me feel better
to think so.

My Mother
Had Another Birthday

She complains
that she does not see
as well as when she was young
She's upset
that she does not hear
as sharply as she used to
She's frustrated
that she can't walk
as fast as she would like to
Yet she exercises every day
she swims
rides her stationary bike
reads the paper daily
goes to concerts
shops for new clothes
walks around the block
plays Scrabble® and bridge
while complaining that
she can't see
can't hear
can't walk
like she used to
many years ago
when she was twenty

My mother does not know
that she's a wonder
a miracle
and to her family and friends
my mother is an inspiration
much admired
and especially
much loved

Miracles

My daughter has a daughter

I have a granddaughter

My mother is a great-grandmother

All miracles

Another Baby

A newborn baby
is so tiny
that it can crawl
right into your heart

A brand-new baby
is so helpless
that you want to protect it
from all of life's hurts

And no matter
how many children
and grandchildren
are in your heart already
there is always room
for one more
to crawl in

Falling in Love
with a Baby

*I saw my tough, cool, macho son
fall in love with a baby this week*

*I saw my somewhat arrogant son
come apart when the baby cried this week*

*I saw my son melt with tenderness
when he watched the baby nurse this week*

*I saw my son overcome with joy
when the baby smiled while sleeping this week*

*I saw my rather fastidious son
change a diaper this week*

*I saw my son
become a father this week*

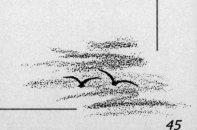

My Granddaughter
Is a Genius

When my granddaughter surprises me
by saying "please" and "thank you"
it seems that this is normal
for a three-year-old

When my granddaughter amazes me
by offering me her cookie
it seems that all three-year-olds
do that, too

When my granddaughter sings a song
almost right on tune
no one seems to find it
extraordinary

When my granddaughter twirls around
in rhythm to the music
no one stops to watch her
with much admiration

Except her grandmother

My Grandson and the Puppy

At first
when my two-year-old grandson
came to stay with us
he was scared of our puppy
and shrieked when she came near
I was afraid
the puppy might bite our grandson

Then
my grandson became bolder
He started teasing the puppy
was more aggressive
and hit her with his toys
I became afraid
my grandson might bite our puppy

The Grandchildren's Visit

The house is ready for them

I have milk and cookies
There are games and toys
Fragile objects are put away
Flower vases are removed

They're here

Cheerful and noisy
they fill the rooms with motion
It's a whirlwind of excitement
We sing and play
We kiss and hug
They leave with presents

They're gone
The house is empty without them

But the house is ready
for me —
with mud on the rugs
jam on the chairs
wet towels on the floor
one shoe under the couch
half-eaten candy in an ashtray
a traumatized dog
and one exhausted
grandmother

Chapter 6

BITS OF WISDOM I'VE LEARNED

*When I was young, I knew the answers;
as I grow older, I know the questions.*

*We do grow wiser with age, and we become more
philosophical. Growing older provides us with the freedom
to be more detached from insignificant events and more
involved with the larger issues.*

*A lifetime of experiences has paved the way for us to trust
our hearts as well as our heads, and to express with
confidence what we always had known to be true.*

The True Secret of Happiness

*Every day have
something to do
or somewhere to go
Every day have
someone to call
someone to see
someone to love
But most important
every day have
something to give
to someone*

Insights and Observations

The secret of longevity is
when you have learned
what to do and
how to do it well
then look for new things
to learn
knowing that at first
you may not do them well

        The way to impress people
        is not by telling them
        how wonderful you are
        If you want to impress people
        you need to listen
        to how wonderful they are

Give your children
more of your presence
instead of more presents

        By trying to be
        everywhere at once
        I am nowhere
        By trying to be
        everything to too many
        I am no one

*Do not look
for the fountain of youth
for you shall search in vain
But drink
from the fountain of love
and you shall find youth*

*Always start the next thing before
you're finished with the last because...
if you wait to be finished with
"have to"
you will never get to
"want to"
and there's even less chance of getting to
"hope to"*

*Most of us after having
spent many years
working to live*

*Spend many more years
living to work*

*And when finally
there is no more work
we don't know how to live*

*Socrates said
"Know thyself"
Let us add:
"Be thyself"
which is much more
difficult to do
because we often are
what others want us to be*

Forget the Ads!

*Are we going to continue
to let the media set the standards
for what we look like
sound like or even act like —
even when it is against our
better judgment?*

*Do we have to look like 15-year-old anorexics
to be considered attractive?
Do we all have to use special creams
so we can age without wrinkles
or alter the color of our hair
to match a shade it used to be?
And what would happen if we stop smiling?*

*I think we should rebel against
face-lifts and hip reductions
hair dyes and anti-wrinkle creams
high-heels that throw our postures out of kilter
girdles that squeeze our middles
and anything that makes us uncomfortable*

*We should accept ourselves as we are —
as women and not teenage models —
and stop obsessing about
each extra pound, new wrinkle
or grey hair*

*We should close the magazines
turn off the TV
stop looking at ads
and just be ourselves*

Inside Out

No matter how old I am on the outside
I am twenty years younger inside

My wrinkled skin covers a youthful one
my grey hair recalls being red

My heavier shape hides a lithe, slender body
my slower step remembers
having a spring in it

No matter how old I am on the outside
there is a vibrant, young woman inside

You Have to Take a Chance

I have known the paths of
failure
frustration
disappointment
defeat

Because I have taken a chance on
winning
succeeding
achieving

It takes a lot of the first
to get some of the second

The Heart Knows

Go where the heart
longs to go
Don't pay attention to the feet
that want to stay rooted

Go where the mind
wants to explore
Don't worry about the hands
that still want to hold on

Go where your gut
is fearful to go
Don't let your body
sit in one place

Go where your heart
knows it should go

Chapter 7

No Regrets

As we grow older, the time we have left grows shorter, and it becomes even more important for us to live fully each day, to appreciate our health, our family, and our friends. No matter how old we are, there are still things to learn, new sights to see, books to read, people to meet and care about.

I used to have red hair
and wore yellow, beige, and green
Now that my hair is grey
I wear bright reds and hot pinks
and look absolutely smashing!

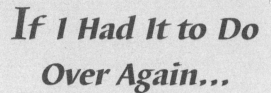

If I Had It to Do Over Again...

In my next life
I will be able to
eat all I want
and not gain weight
play the guitar
and sing
get a medical degree
and find the cure for cancer
Otherwise
I wouldn't change a thing

Sometimes I Forget

Sometimes
when I dial a phone number
by the time someone answers
I forget who it was I was calling

Sometimes
when I write a note to myself
to answer a call or a letter
I forget where I put it

Sometimes
when I leave the house
I forget whether I left the lights on
or turned the stove off

Sometimes
I have to check if my toothbrush is wet
to know whether I had already
brushed my teeth that morning

Sometimes
on my way home
I drive right by my house
and only notice it a few blocks later

Sometimes
I forget whether I meant to say something
or whether I have already said it

But often
I remember the kind words
the sweet smells
sunlit days
a tender touch
a book I loved
music, a picture
a special event

I guess I remember more than I forget

I Know Who I Am

*I don't have to flirt
be cute, fun, charming
wear heels
and rely on my looks
to attract men*

*I don't have to worry
about cellulite on my thighs
or pushing up my breasts
or the tan line of my bikini*

*I don't have to wonder
anymore
about what I will be
when I grow up*

*I can be outrageous
powerful
say what I think
not fear anyone
stand up for what I believe*

*I can be
who I am!*

I'm Not Climbing Ladders Anymore

I have discovered the joy
of caring less
about success
about visibility and significance
about what others think of me
about how I sound

I have given up on rinses for grey hair
on the creams that don't help wrinkles
I have finally accepted
that those extra pounds
will probably be a part of me forever
I can overlook being overlooked

I do not need to see all the sights
when I travel
I can miss a cathedral or a museum
and take a nap in my hotel room instead
I don't have to go to every good movie
or read the books on the bestseller lists

I'm not climbing any ladders
I'm not fighting for center stage
I'm not competing for any favors
I don't owe anyone anything

And as I watch others
struggle for a place in the sun
I can sit peacefully in the twilight
doing my needlepoint
enjoying a quiet talk
with a big mug of hot tea

Sunday

I sit in my garden
a dish on my lap
with a big scoop of chocolate ice cream

My feet in the sun
my head in the shade
my eyes on the distant horizon

I worked hard all week
I answered my mail
and my desk is not in a clutter

I talked to my mother
called up the kids
and straightened the drawers and closets

I sewed a loose button
tightened a screw
and finished last Sunday's papers

I even made up
our bed today
although no company's coming

All this is to say
that I really deserve
that scoop of chocolate ice cream

I'm Grateful for the Little Things

I listen to the silence
I am grateful that
in these times of noise pollution
I have a quiet room

I breathe the air
I am grateful that
in these times of air pollution
I have a fragrant garden

I take a walk
I am grateful that
I don't have an illness
that limits my activities

I sit quietly with friends
I am grateful that
in these times of rushing around
I can take time out
take time off
take the time
to be grateful for
these little things
and celebrate my life
as a "gift"
not as a "given"

Blessings Counted

I want to thank my parents
for having made me
daughter

I want to thank my husband
for having made me
wife

I am thanking my children
for making me
mother

and their children
for I am now
grandma

I want to thank young people
for letting me be
teacher

And I thank all those
who are calling me
friend

But most of all
I'm thankful
that I can appreciate
all of the above

ABOUT THE AUTHOR

Natasha Josefowitz calls herself a late bloomer, having earned her master's degree at age 40 and her Ph.D. at age 50. She is an adjunct professor at the School of Social Work at San Diego State University, a noted columnist, and the author of three books on management, eight books of humorous verse, a book for children, and a book for couples.

Dr. Josefowitz is an internationally known speaker, having lived and worked abroad and in the U.S. Her efforts on behalf of women have earned her numerous awards, including **The Living Legacy Award** from the Women's International Center and **The Women Helping Women Award** from the Soroptimist International. She has been named **Woman of the Year** five times by various national and international organizations, including the Women's Management Association, and was also honored by California Women in Government for her contributions to education.

Natasha is the mother and stepmother of five children and has seven grandchildren and step-grandchildren. She is grey-haired, wrinkled, and has a few extra pounds, but says she can celebrate life because she has PMZ (Post-Menopausal Zest).

In a Nutshell

More can be said
in fewer words
in verse
But more important
more can be heard